WHAT IS THE ELECTORAL COLLEGE?

BALLOT

VOTE

BY SANTANA HUNT

Gareth Stevens
PUBLISHING

CRASHCOURSE

Please visit our website, www.garethstevens.com. For a free color catalog of all our high-quality books, call toll free 1-800-542-2595 or fax 1-877-542-2596.

Cataloging-in-Publication Data
Names: Hunt, Santana.
Title: What Is the electoral college? / Santana Hunt.
Description: New York : Gareth Stevens Publishing, 2018. | Series: A look at your government | Includes index.
Identifiers: ISBN 9781482460636 (pbk.) | ISBN 9781482460650 (library bound) | ISBN 9781482460643 (6 pack) |
Subjects: LCSH: Electoral college--United States--Juvenile literature. | Presidents--United States--Election--Juvenile literature. | United States--Politics and government--Juvenile literature.
Classification: LCC JK529.H83 2018 | DDC 324.6'3--dc23

First Edition

Published in 2018 by
Gareth Stevens Publishing
111 East 14th Street, Suite 349
New York, NY 10003

Copyright © 2018 Gareth Stevens Publishing

Editor: Kristen Nelson
Designer: Samantha DeMartin

Photo credits: Series art MaxyM/Shutterstock.com; cover, pp. 1, 30 (map) Electric Crayon/DigitalVision Vectors/Getty Images; cover, p. 1 (voting box) Daniel Hurst Photography/Photographer's Choice/Getty Images; p. 5 MarshalN20/Wikimedia Commons; p. 7 Saul Loeb/AFP/Getty Images; p. 9 Robert King/Hulton Archive/Getty Images; p. 11 Alex Wong/Getty Images News/Getty Images; p. 13 South12th Photography/Shutterstock.com; p. 15 Bettmann/Bettmann/Getty Images; p. 17 Joseph Sohm/Shutterstock.com; p. 19 Joseph August/Shutterstock.com; p. 21 Hill Street Studios/Blend Images/Getty Images; p. 23 (both) k2 images/Shutterstock.com; p. 25 PAUL J. RICHARDS/AFP/Getty Images; p. 27 Kathryn Scott Osler/Denver Post/Getty Images; p. 29 Gino Santa Maria/Shutterstock.com; p. 30 Mike McDonald/Shutterstock.com.

Printed in the United States of America

CPSIA compliance information: Batch #CS17GS: For further information contact Gareth Stevens, New York, New York at 1-800-542-2595.

CONTENTS

The Process   4

By the Numbers   6

Who Is an Elector?   8

Our Votes, Their Votes   12

Popular or Electoral?   18

A Winner!   22

Change Ahead?   26

Electoral Votes by State   30

Glossary   31

For More Information   32

Index   32

Words in the glossary appear in **bold** type the first time they are used in the text.

THE PROCESS

The Electoral College isn't a place. It's the **process** by which a group of people called electors cast votes for the US president and vice president. The highest law in the United States, the Constitution, created this process.

MAKE THE GRADE

Some Founding Fathers wanted to let the voters choose their president, and others wanted to let Congress vote. The Electoral College was a **compromise**.

5

By the Numbers

Congress is made up of the Senate and the House of **Representatives**. Each state is **allotted** a number of electors equal to its number of House representatives and senators. The Electoral College is made up of 538 electors. Each elector equals one electoral vote.

JOINT SESSION OF CONGRESS

MAKE THE GRADE

Washington, DC, isn't a state, but it has three electoral votes according to the Twenty-Third **Amendment** to the US Constitution.

WHO IS AN ELECTOR?

The Constitution doesn't say who can be an elector. Electors are commonly political party leaders within each state. They're often people who work for the state government or who have some connection to a presidential **candidate**.

MAKE THE GRADE

A political party is a group of people who share beliefs about how a government should be run.

How electors are chosen depends on the laws of the state they're from. Most often, the candidate's political party chooses electors. Each presidential candidate has a group of electors in each state ready to vote for them.

MAKE THE GRADE

The Constitution says members of Congress can't be electors. It's not as clearly written, but many understand the Constitution to say other national government workers can't be electors either.

11

OUR VOTES, THEIR VOTES

The US presidential **election** happens every 4 years on the Tuesday after the first Monday in November. But when people vote, they're actually voting for their candidate's electors! Some states even list electors' names under the candidates' names.

PRESIDENT AND VICE PRESIDENT
PRESIDENTE Y VICEPRESIDENTE

Vote for One Party
Vote por Un Partido

RALPH NADER
for President \para Presidente
MATT GONZALEZ
for Vice President \para Vicepresidente

Peace and
Freedom
Paz y Libertad

BARACK OBAMA
for President \para Presidente
JOE BIDEN
for Vice President \para Vicepresidente

Democratic
Demócrata

BOB BARR
for President \para Presidente
WAYNE A. ROOT
for Vice President \para Vicepresidente

Libertarian
Libertario

JOHN MCCAIN
for President \para Presidente
SARAH PALIN
for Vice President \para Vicepresidente

Republican
Republicano

CYNTHIA MCKINNEY
for President \para Presidente
ROSA CLEMENTE
for Vice President \para Vicepresidente

Green
Verde

ALAN KEYES
for President \para Presidente
WILEY S. DRA...
for Vice Presi...

MAKE THE GRADE

After the election, state governors prepare special papers stating who will be the electors for the state.

13

Washington, DC, and 48 of the US states award all their electoral votes to the candidate who wins the **popular vote** in the state. In Nebraska and Maine, the electoral votes can be split between candidates.

MAKE THE GRADE

Awarding all the electoral votes to one candidate is called the "winner-take-all" allotment of votes.

PRESIDENT RONALD REAGAN
WON THE POPULAR VOTE AND
489 ELECTORAL VOTES IN 1980

15

On the Monday following the second Wednesday in December, electors meet in their state. Each elector casts one vote for president and one for vice president. Candidates need 270 electoral votes to win. That's one more than half of the total.

MAKE THE GRADE

Electors often meet in their state's capital.

17

POPULAR OR ELECTORAL?

The candidate who wins the popular vote will commonly win the electoral vote. However, some states have more electoral votes than others. A candidate doesn't need to win electoral votes from all states. They can win with the votes of fewer than half the states!

PRESIDENT GEORGE W. BUSH
LOST THE POPULAR VOTE BUT WON
THE ELECTORAL VOTE IN 2000

MAKE THE GRADE

In 1876, 1888, and 2000, presidents who won enough electoral votes but lost the popular vote were elected.

19

Some states' laws say electors must vote for the candidate who won the popular vote. Other electors pledge, or promise, their political party they will vote for their candidate. It's uncommon for an elector to cast a vote different than expected.

MAKE THE GRADE

While states have laws about it, there's no US government law stating that electors must vote according to the popular vote of their state.

21

A WINNER!

The Electoral College votes are counted in Congress on January 6 of the year following the November election. The current vice president then reads the outcome of the electoral votes for president and vice president.

MAKE THE GRADE

Today, presidents run with a vice presidential candidate as a "running mate." Running mates are elected together, though votes are cast separately.

PRESIDENT
BARACK OBAMA

VICE PRESIDENT
JOE BIDEN

23

What happens if no candidate has 270 electoral votes? The US Constitution states that the presidential election is decided by a vote in the House of Representatives. The Senate votes to elect the vice president.

MAKE THE GRADE

The House chooses from the three presidential candidates with the most electoral votes.

25

CHANGE AHEAD?

Since the early 1800s, a Constitutional amendment changing the Electoral College process has been brought up more than 700 times! Some people want to vote directly for the president and let the popular vote decide who wins.

MAKE THE GRADE

The Electoral College process makes it hard for someone running in a smaller political party to win the presidency.

The Electoral College has elected the president and vice president for more than 200 years. It's possible that the Electoral College will be changed someday—or done away with completely! Until then, it will continue to do its job.

MAKE THE GRADE

Amending the Constitution is a long, hard process. That's likely why any amendments about the Electoral College haven't passed.

ELECTORAL VOTES
BY STATE

WA 11
OR 7
MT 3
ND 3
MN 10
ME 4
ID 4
SD 3
WI 10
VT 3
NH 4
MA 12
WY 3
MI 17
NY 31
NV 5
IA 7
PA 21
RI 4
UT 5
CO 9
NE 5
IL 21
IN 11
OH 11
CT 7
DE 3
CA 55
KS 6
MO 11
KY 8
WV 5
VA 13
MD 10
DC 3
AZ 10
NM 5
OK 7
AR 6
TN 11
NC 15
TX 34
LA 9
MS 6
AL 9
GA 15
SC 8
FL 27
AK 3
HI 4

TOTAL ELECTORAL VOTES: 538
VOTES NEEDED TO WIN: 270

I VOTED

30

GLOSSARY

allot: to give a part to

amendment: a change or addition to a constitution

candidate: someone who runs for a position

compromise: a way of two sides reaching agreement in which each gives up something to end an argument

election: the act of voting someone into a government position

popular vote: the votes cast by those allowed to vote

process: a series of steps or actions taken to complete something

representative: a member of a lawmaking body who acts for voters

FOR MORE INFORMATION

BOOKS

Grayson, Robert. *Voters: From Primaries to Decision Night.* Minneapolis, MN: Lerner Publishing Group, 2016.

Harper, Leslie. *How Do Elections Work?* New York, NY: PowerKids Press, 2013.

WEBSITES

Elections 101

pbskids.org/zoom/fromyou/elections/elections101.html

Review the voting process and why it's important to take part in it.

Publisher's note to educators and parents: Our editors have carefully reviewed these websites to ensure that they are suitable for students. Many websites change frequently, however, and we cannot guarantee that a site's future contents will continue to meet our high standards of quality and educational value. Be advised that students should be closely supervised whenever they access the Internet.

INDEX

amendment 7, 26, 28

compromise 5

Congress 5, 6, 10, 22

Constitution 4, 7, 8, 10, 24, 28

election 12, 13, 22, 24

electoral vote 6, 7, 14, 16, 18, 19, 22, 24, 30

electors 4, 6, 8, 10, 12, 13, 16, 20

House of Representatives 6, 24

political party 8, 9, 10, 20, 27

popular vote 14, 18, 19, 20, 26

Senate 6, 24